THE ARMCHAIR *to*

by KEN COLLINGS

TAKE THAT BOOKS

Take That Books is an imprint of
Take That Ltd.
P.O.Box 200
Harrogate
HG1 4XB

Copyright © 1994 Take That Books

Written by Ken Collings
with thanks to Dave Harper
Illustrated by Clyde

Australian Associate:
MaxiBooks, P.O.Box 529, Kiama, NSW 2533, Australia.

10 9 8 7 6 5 4 3 2 1

All rights reserved around the world. This publication is copyright and may not be reproduced in whole or in part in any manner (except excerpts thereof for bona fide purposes in accordance with the Copyright Act) without the prior consent in writing from the publisher.

This is a work of humour and of fiction. Under no circumstances should anybody act on material given in this book. The publisher, author, and their respective employees or agents, shall not accept responsibility for injury, loss or damage occasioned by any person acting or refraining from action as a result of material in this book whether or not such injury, loss or damage is in any way due to any negligent act or omission, breach of duty or default on the part of the publisher, author, or their respective employees or agents.

ISBN 1-873668-12-0

Layout and typesetting by
Impact Design, P.O.Box 200, Harrogate, HG1 4XB.

Printed and bound in Great Britain.

HAPPINES IS A ROD IN YOUR HAND

THE CATCH OF A LIFETIME

Most anglers fantasise about catching a big fish of one type or another. But what they are really after is the ultimate catch of a lifetime, the one they dream about every single night.

It is the most attractive and desirable specimen you could ever imagine and its vital statistics are 38:24:36 - yes, a real life mermaid. Known to frequent the River Trent and a few local duck ponds, this voluptuous specimen is believed to be the offspring of a fanatical angler and his horny wife.

Indeed the last reported landings were by an 80-year-old angler from the River Trent at Fiskerton who apparently returned it as he didn't know what to do with it. Poor old sausage.

Good specimens are extremely difficult to land possibly because of the strange shape of their body. Perhaps this is the reason why mermaid hunting brigades use gigantic landing nets.

Well known tabloid newspapers and top shelf magazines are reported to have offered a massive reward to any angler who lands a genuine mermaid over 100 lb. So, anyone fortunate enough to land one of these variety could make themselves a fortune. If you fancy a go, the most popular bait is a crumpled £50 note and a bunch of diamonds glued to a size 6 hook.

Please note, great care should be taken when handling this species as they are known to be extremely aggressive...

RELAX! GO FISHING?

"Relax, go fishing," said the doctor to a man suffering from stress related ulcers.

He's got to be joking, hasn't be? I bet he's never tried getting up at the crack of dawn in the depths of winter after the habitual Saturday night curry and eighteen pints of lager!

Mouth like a sewer, throbbing head, brain dead, are you sure? Even work is better than this, thank you very much.

WEATHER

No matter what the weather conditions, they are always the wrong sort for good fishing! Never a day goes past when the average angler blames the sun, or lack of it, for slow sport. And the old wives tale about rain being good for fishing receives the same treatment.

Hot weather also plays havoc with the bait. Maggots are pretty hardy creatures, but a couple of hours in the hot sun does them no good at all. First they wriggle like mad and then they stop wriggling, cos they are dead. Yes, dear reader, the inside of a maggot is like an egg and they fry like eggs too. All those pints of bait wiped out because you left that heavy old umbrella in the car. Don't you feel gutted?

Worse still is the rain when uncovered bait manages to defy gravity.

All maggots take the opportunity of a downpour to make an escape, but the champion climber of them all is The Pinkie better known as the offspring of the greenbottle.

There is nowhere these little varmints cannot climb. Your nice bait stand is infested with these tiny maggots and before you know it, they find shelter in your tackle bag.

Two months later when you next go fishing, you open up your bag and vrooom - out flies hundreds of angry greenbottles. This is even more embarrassing when your beloved wife, who you give a lift to the shops on the way to the river, decides to slip a Mars bar in your bag!

THE TACKLE SHOP

To the average angler, the tackle shop is an Aladdin's Cave. It is virtually impossible to go into one and come out without having been relieved of your betting winnings.

A typical tackle shop greets you like a Sumo Wrestler's armpit as the waft of the maggots hits you. But how most fishermen have grown to love that smell.

Regulars are congregated around the counter with cups of tea (served in vessels that aren't even clean enough for the Greasy Spoon Cafe).

All are giving it the big one, about how they are going to do the business tomorrow. Getting round them is like an obstacle course on the Krypton Factor as you have to negotiate the buckets of maggots round their feet.

All this changes as you approach the carp department, alias Headbangers Corner. Here the smell changes to the sickly sweet. You'd think you were in a positer's parlour. God help the poor fish. It always looks more like a chemist than a tackle shop, with bottles of potions and powders of all different colours and flavours.

HAZARDS

It is well known in the television world that you never get involved with animals or children. Sadly they are both prolific in angling. But animals usually cause the most concern.

Take a well known angler who was fishing on the River Mole at Cobham in a winter league match. In those days, equipment was carefully put on the ground behind the angler. Our hero felt a nudge on his shoulder and looked round to see a horse's face six inches from his right hand ear. The horse looked stupidly at the angler who jumped in alarm. This made the horse jump... all over the poor angler's £1,000 roach pole. To add insult to injury the horse ran off with the angler's favourite chicken sandwiches.

Sheep also can be a pain in the butt, with the same unfortunate angler being visited by a rogue ram who took a fancy to his nice smelly continental groundbait! Over £10 worth was swiftly devoured whilst the irate owner, stuck in the mud, tried in vain to shoo it away.

But the worst irritant of all is the dreaded cow. They are so nosey and only a soft whack on the head with a bank stick seems to get the message through - at least for five minutes anyway. They also take delight in trampling over your favourite rod and leaving their calling cards all around your swim.

This normally friendly beast can inadvertently take on another form after dark. And many a carp angler has had a rude awakening when a friendly bovine has tried to share a bivvy with its dopey occupant.

SUPER SALESMAN

Every tackle shop has got one. With him in the shop, you go in for a half pint of maggots and come out with an armful of tackle and empty pockets.

Still, at least they soften you up first with a cup of tea and a nice chat about fishing. They are really keen to hear about your latest exploits and come up with some great ideas on how to get even more fish on the bank.

Of course, this usually involves you having to buy the latest hot rod. It is lighter, has a sweeter action and only costs £50 more than the one you bought last season. "This rod really is the business," he proclaims. Funny that, didn't he say the same thing just six months ago?

Naturally you will need a suitable holdall to put your super new rod in.

In the old days a piece of string would have done the job. But now you need a flashy super-dooper model which contains more drainpipes than a country mansion. It is made out of the finest materials known to man and is, of course, once again extremely expensive!

The new tackle box he tries to sell you is a real wonder to behold. The all singing, all dancing, model has finally arrived. For only £500 (plus 17½% VAT, and £100 extra for the bells and whistles) you can purchase a look-a-like Lunar Landing Module. As well as carrying fishing tackle, it will look good as a piece of furniture in the front room. It can also be used as a cigar box, and if really necessary, you could even sit on it!

Thank goodness he doesn't sell brushes on the doorstep or, even worse, insurance!

MAGIC MOMENTS

Never mind Dennis Norden and "It'll be All Right on the Night", there have been some even more magical cock-ups in angling.

Take the man who was caught short, really desperate for a number twos in the middle of winter, and all togged up in his one piece suit.

It happened to a chap, who to spare his blushes, we will call John, 'cos that was his name. One day at a big match, with spectators galore, and little natural cover, the call of nature came.

Now, when you have to go, you have to go! So, there is a very simple system that can be employed, and it's called desperation: You drop 'em, do it and pull 'em up all in one movement. And this is exactly what John did. Then he swaggered back to his swim, sporting a big smile and huge sigh of relief.

Unbeknown to our hero, what should have been dumped in the undergrowth was in fact delicately placed in his hood! All was well until it started to rain. And you can guess the rest.

The moral of the story: ALWAYS check to see if it's where it should be!

POLEITIS

Poleitis is sweeping the country, it is highly contagious and once contracted you are hooked for life. Symptoms are an uncontrollable desire to fish at 13 metres or even longer, excruciating back pain and a very large bank overdraft, none of which is a very pleasant experience. There is no known cure for this terrible affliction, so be warned!

Whoever said that fishing is "a worm at one end and a fool on the other" must have been describing a pole angler. Who else would sit and hold a great big 14 metre pole all day, especially when most of the fish are probably swimming around under your feet.

Using a pole on the canal towpath must rank as one of the world's most hazardous elements of fishing. If the towpath cyclists or motorcyclists don't get you, then the joggers almost certainly will. Even if these idiots don't smash your beautiful pole to smithereens, rest assured you will have to contend with a dollop of dog's doo that seems to always cake the part of the pole you actually wish to hold.

All in all, if you can negotiate the boats, joggers, cyclists and old grannies who insist on feeding the water fowl in your swim, and still enjoy catching gudgeon you definitely have the terminal disease.

WINTER MADNESS

Some anglers suffer severe withdrawal symptoms if they find themselves unable to go fishing, and will often go to extraordinary lengths in order to wet a line.

Heaven help the poor wife and kids of the angler who is unable to get his weekly fix. Even in the depths of winter this desperate need prevails. Despite freezing temperatures and sheeting rain, he will still go out knowing full well that even with eight layers of clothing, ski boots and a woolly hat, the cold will still get to him. Even a slug of whisky doesn't seem to work for long.

The prospect of six inches of ice doesn't even bother our intrepid hero. For he is probably carrying the standard ice breaking kit, consisting of a brick and chain, or more impressively, a chain saw. With this he can make a hole in the ice to dangle his float and thus satisfy his craving. Frozen fingers and toes are quickly forgotten as he triumphantly plucks the first fish of the day from the tiny opening.

There is of course a limit to this madness as many night anglers can testify. After a long session on a bitterly cold night, these masochists often awaken to find their lines frozen solid and their landing nets like giant tennis rackets.

Is there a downside to all this? Well, perhaps the angler will have to spend a week in bed recovering from pneumonia and frostbite. But he won't mind, just as long as he is fit for next week's trip. After all, you do have to get life in perspective, don't you!

THE BAILIFF

The Gestapo are alive and living on the banks of the river, that's for sure. No sooner have you cast out than he is there, demanding day-ticket money with menaces. Not content with that, he has to tell you that you are fishing like a willy.

Whatever you do don't offer him a £20 note for a two quid day-ticket. This will give him the hump to such a degree that he'll insist you reel in your tackle and inspect every item. Still not content, he may then delve into your bag and find the dreaded tin can!

Now, a tin of luncheon meat to most people is quite harmless. But not to the zealous bigot confronting you. He'll grab you by the scruff of your neck and frog-march you off the fishery in front of all your mates, and warn you of impending peril before The Committee for taking a tin on the water.

And you just want a quiet day out, away from the trouble and strife. Oh well, such is life!

A PERFECT DAY

My wife tells me that my life consists of the three Fs: Fishing, Food and F........, er, Fornicating. Not I might add, necessarily in that order. If this is living, what will heaven be like?

THE COACH OUTING

Traditional club outings once revolved around the fortnightly coach trip. These have all but vanished now due to the increase in private motor cars. But, for the few clubs that still run coaches, they cause nothing but problems. Each trip is generally poorly supported and consequently runs at a massive loss. Those who have the audacity to challenge the wisdom of these losses, at annual general meetings, are firmly put in their place as the old brigade try and cling to tradition.

Nevertheless, coach trips have always had their own special charm, haven't they?...

As you stand shivering at the pickup for what seems like hours, you muse whether the driver has been on the booze and overslept again. Then, just as you begin to despair, out of the early morning mist and sounding like a steam locomotive, appears the old banger of a vehicle. It has probably seen over 20 years of service and really belongs in the knackers yard.

Charlie the driver greets you with his usual friendly glare and grumpily informs you there had better be no maggots aboard and warns you, "don't lean your rods against the coach, sonny". He watches disapprovingly as you struggle to fit 40 sets of tackle into a six foot square boot, and then cops the strop as you have to take half the kit inside the coach. Mind you, he is going to moan a lot more on the homeward trip when everything is caked in mud and maggots. Still he has to earn his tip somehow, doesn't he?

The coach hasn't even pulled away before the card shark pulls out his battered pack of cards, intent on fleecing all and sundry of their spare dosh. He usually manages to succeed well before arrival at the destination.

The homeward trip is of course far more memorable. Forget the fishing, which is usually poor anyway, the booze up is far more important! Despite Charlie's protests, the party staggers back on to the coach with cans of booze and bags of chips. Then the antics begin. If you thought a full moon was only once a month, then think again! Many a fishing coach has decorated its rear window with hairy bums!

The coach finally arrives home and even Charlie has to smile as he thinks of spending his bag of 2p coins (and buttons) given as tip money. The smelly but happy band of anglers lurch off the coach and head for home, another good day had by all. Long live the coach trip.

THE COMMITTEE

Rules are there to be broken, of course. But transgress in a club match and a fate worse than death awaits you! Yes, its a trip in front of the dreaded Committee - a fate which strikes fear into even the boldest of men.

The alleged offender is hauled up before a line of wizened old men to explain his actions. Which, of course, is a pointless exercise because he has already been found guilty as charged.

He is then subjected to a torrent of verbal abuse as he stands with head bowed prior to being sentenced. No matter that a can of beer was found by an over zealous official, snooping in the accused's box, when its owner had gone to answer the call of nature. Cans and bottles are banned, simple as that.

Sentence is pronounced, and the guilty party is forced to hand in his rule book and badge for a whole season. Still it could be worse, the penalty for leaving litter at a club fishery is being hung, drawn and quartered.

Never mind, one day you may on The Committee and be blessed with Draconian powers. Won't you have fun then?

TAKING THE BAIT

THE WORMER

Gathering lobworms in the middle of the night from the local golf course can, at times, be a very hazardous occupation.

Much stealth, speed and bravery is required since the humble lobworm is nobody's fool. He has an equal desire to pull you screaming down his hole as you have to pull him out of it. A fact highlighted by the large number of lobworm gatherers who have mysteriously disappeared during the past few years. They have presumably been gobbled up by a bunch of greedy lobs anxious to avenge the disappearance of their own colleagues.

Generally the result of this unsupervised tug-of-war is an honourable draw. The lob will slither through your fingers back to the safety of its hole to nurse his swollen head, whilst you skulk off in search of another likely victim.

Other hazards in worm gathering are rather closer to home. Many an angler has been the subject of close questioning by a member of the local constabulary after being discovered on the 18th green in dubious clothing complete with a bucket, rubber gloves and tapping stick. Be prepared, you may get your collar felt when you embark on this dead of the night exercise. So have your excuses ready and make sure you know where the nearest fancy dress party is being held. Otherwise make sure you have your toothbrush with you as they don't have them in police cells.

MAGGOT FARM

You could be forgiven for thinking that it was a prison. But that remote, imposing building is in fact far worse - it is the maggot farm. Downwind, on a sunny day in June, the smell can knock you out at five miles.

A visit is like a trip to hell. Even the prospect of a cheap gallon of maggots is not worth the ordeal.

As you arrive, you think that you are playing the part of an extra in a Hitchcock film. Blackbirds the size of vultures circle the building eagerly watching for their meal. Once in the door, you then have to negotiate the fly house. Five million flies will immediately dive bomb you and try to fly up your left nostril. When they've finished with that orifice, they'll start looking for another. And if you are not careful, they'll even find holes you didn't know you had!

On the sieves lye carcasses of chickens, beef burgers and even British Rail sandwiches - anything to feed the ravenous maggot. At the far side of the building is the area where the maggots are cleaned off for sale to the punters. Hand over your fiver to the smiling hooded ghoul, pick up your five pint 'gallon', and get out of there quickly before they use you as bait!

THE SLUG MAN

For most anglers the humble maggot is still the number one bait. But there are those amongst us who prefer, for some peculiar reason, to use something a little more exotic like the humble slug. Yes the ordinary black common-or-garden jobs. Yuk!

Collecting them is bad enough, and keen gardeners can talk aplenty about the slug patrol. But to have to put them on hook, and actually fish with them is something else. Just picking them out of the bait box gives you the willies. And as for that gooey slime, well you cannot get it off your fingers can you, no matter how hard you try and lick. Apparently though the chub find them absolutely irresistible, they just love sticky ones with juicy soft centres - there is really no accounting for taste is there?

Some people insist, that in exotic parts of the world, slugs are regarded as a delicacy and gourmets will pay a fortune for a mere plateful. Somehow though, 'Sweet and Sour Slugs' doesn't seem to ring true, and in any event they would probably stick to the roof of your mouth wouldn't they!

MEET THEM ON THE BANK

THE CLUB CHAMPION

Only bigheads ever apply for this title. You can spot them a mile off; Angling Times Club Champion cloth badges galore on their coat, and numerous trophies proudly displayed on the telly.

The 'champion' swaggers on to the bank each week with an air of confidence - although many feel he carries a different sort of aroma.

All the other club members would just love to knock him down a peg. But at the end of the day, the real sickener is that you'll always find he's gone and won again. And the prize money means he'll be able to buy even more fancy tackle.

And finally, to make matters even worse, everyone has to endure his puffed out chest and his bragging all the way home. What a sad person!

THE FLY FISHERMAN

Everyone knows this one. Dressed like a right wally, silly hat, plus fours, a waistcoat with more pockets than Batman's utility belt and of course the mandatory Hunter boots. All topped off with a clipped accent

This fine specimen of an angler, of course, prefers to be addressed as "The Colonel". As for his tackle, you will observe that the rods are ultra thin and light, but the line is like the hawser used on a cross channel ferry. The patterns of flies he carries are a wonder to behold, yet he cannot even undo the ones on his own pants.

There is, of course, only one thing sillier than a trout angler. Yes, you've guessed it - the trout.

ANOTHER PERFECT DAY

Hardened sea anglers see newcomers every year attempt to gain their spurs as they go offshore for the first time.

But for the newcomer this first trip can be a nightmare. All is well in the harbour but as soon as the boat leaves the shelter of the wall, then all hell breaks loose and it is like being on a bucking bronco.

Ten miles out to sea and the motor stops and the skipper lowers the anchor. Still the boat tosses up and down and the nightmare continues. But in a new act of bravery our debutante tries to start fishing only to overrun his reel by forgetting to put his thumb on the spool. A massive birds nest follows, which incurs the wrath of his companions, as terminal tackle tangles up.

The greasy breakfast is first to appear, hopefully over the side of the boat, followed by much moaning and asking for God's assistance. But, even the seagulls ignore this unauthorised groundbaiting.

No amount of whinging affects the duration of the trip as the other seven anglers look smugly on at this poor wretch with a green face grovelling in the pit of the boat. What is he, a man or a mouse?

Eventually the ordeal is nearly over and the boat is steaming back to the harbour. Most of the party have caught some nice cod and whiting, but what has our friend got to show for his efforts? Only a couple of lousy pouting which even the cat won't touch. It's a good job there is a wet fish shop on the way home!

FISH FACE

Talk about some owners looking like their dogs. Have you ever seen the face of a carp angler? Pouting mouth, bulging eyes, scaley skin, whiskers and a hooter like a rhinoceros, you certainly wouldn't want to fish next to him at night

He even has a habit and a bad one at that. He just cannot stop munching boilies. He chomps his way through a bulk bag every session. His favourite flavour is Tutti Fruity (it couldn't be anything else could it?)!

You can also smell him a mile off, as he tests his new flavours by using them as a body deodorant, which makes him pong like a strawberry farm. Mind you, it could be a lot worse, it could be seafood flavour! Phew!

RAINBOW HAZARDS

Even an experienced trout angler sometimes finds that the sport can have its painful moments. And one old boy found out what the saying 'hooked on fly fishing' really meant!

Not content with catching the tree behind him several times, he caught something even more excruciating. On one of the few occasions he actually got the line in the water, he hooked something solid. A gentle

tug and then thwack! A size ten hook with all the trimmings went straight into the tip of his nose!

After several attempts with a pair of pliers to remove the Bloody Butcher fly from his hooter, the amateur surgeon (who made Jack the Ripper seem tame!), then suggested the fly could be removed in hospital when they'd finished the day's fishing. The screaming victim protested vehemently, much to the amusement of other anglers and the bemused fishery owner. Much to the sufferer's relief, they relented and drove him to the casualty department at Chichester Hospital where the fly was removed.

Poor fellow, not only did he have to endure the removal of the hook but also the added embarrassment of receiving a tetanus jab. Funny how the place fills with nurses when you drop your trousers, isn't it!

Who would want to go fly fishing?!?

THE BEACH ANGLER

You cannot mistake the beach angler. There he is wandering down the promenade adorned with silly bobble hat, oiled-wool sweater, and chest waders. A rod in one hand and a bucket of worms in the other, he carefully avoids the other users and spikes his rod rest into the beach at the edge of the surf. Watch out, this angler is a killer, a danger to both man and beast.

He carefully attaches his 6oz lead, complete with sharpened spikes and proceeds to wind himself up for a big chuck. Looking like a cross between a Morris Dancer and Geoff Capes he faces the promenade and swings round casting his rod in an arc, only to fall flat on his face. He's failed to notice the little boy who has carefully attached his hook to the nearby groyne!

Red faced he shoos the irritating brat away and repeats the exercise, only to hear a rifle like crack as the lead snaps off and propels itself in the direction of the pier 50 yards along the beach. The sound of crashing glass is shortly followed by the sight of sixty old biddies standing on the pier platform shaking their fists. Once again their Bingo session has been ruined by a flying lead which has come to rest in the ceiling of the 100 year old hall.

THE CRAFTY CATCHER

You meet them in all walks of life and fishing is no exception. Whether its adding stones to the weighbag at the Xmas sweepstake, or craftily slipping a prime trout down your wellie to take home for supper. There is always someone who will try and beat the system

The ever watchful fishery manager is always on the look out for these shady characters. But he's up against stiff opposition.

The 'put and take' fisheries are a particular challenge for the would be crafty catcher. If maggots and bread slipped on to the fly don't work, he can always resort to plundering the stock pond.

The boat angler also has methods of his own such as "accidentally" allowing his line to fall into the water and catch by trolling whilst rowing to the far side. This ruse even fools the most eagle eyed bailiff.

Trout are so stupid that sometimes a four-fish limit is reached within half an hour of starting. What do you do then? Hiding the fish used to be an option but nowadays many bailiffs walk round with sniffer dogs specially trained to retrieve fish and also identify the culprit who concealed them. There you are quietly fishing away when this pooch wanders up with fish in its gob and pees on your boot to show its irate owner that you are the guilty party'

KING CARP

Now we all know that the average carp angler rarely catches anything. But when he does, the fish is treated like royalty. From the moment it slides gently into the soft-as-silk, oversized landing net, which is big enough to land an elephant, it is given more attention than the Prime Minister gives to a visiting dignitary.

Not for the carp a mere grass bank or gravel path which lesser fish have to suffer. Instead it is laid gently on a cross between a water bed and blow up doll. There the hook is carefully removed using precision surgical instruments (sterilised of course) and antiseptic is applied to the slight prick mark.

The fish is lovingly caressed, kissed and cuddled and then photographed from every conceivable angle (after of course the captor has brushed his hair, applied his make up and made sure his sponsor's logo is more

prominently displayed than on a Formula 1 racer). Vital statistics such as weight, girth and length are carefully noted, while scale patterns reveal if the fish is a "known name".

And what names they are given! Clarissa, The Parrot, Two-Tone, Lumpy, Jack the Lad, Shoulders and Strawberry. One is even named Lady Chatterly, which leaves little to the imagination. What will happen when a carp angler gets her in to his hairy arms? Oh to be a carp!

THE EXPERT

There you are sat quietly on the riverbank, soaking up the sun, aimlessly watching the wild life and taking in the lovely countryside, and maybe even catching the occasional lucky fish. Oh what a pleasant way to spend the day.

But what is that thumping along the bank, loaded to the gunnels with tackle and bait?

Oh no! It is the dreaded expert. The very last person you wish to see. Observing that you have a few fish in your keepnet, he promptly plonks himself down as close as he possibly can without sticking his bankstick in your left earhole.

Out comes his manual and after much buffing, puffing and swearing, he somehow manages to assemble his lunar module, which incidentally doubles as a tackle box. Out of his bag comes a baby's bath along with a sack of brown crumb. He mixes this lot up and then adds water plus enough maggots to cause an outbreak of Black Death.

After five minutes, the brew has turned into concrete and the bombardment begins. Not since World War Two has there been such a Hiatus in this part of the world. His efforts are unselfish, with much of the mix landing squarely in your swim, scattering the remaining fish from your peg.

Oh well, musn't grumble, all in a day's fishing!

Then to add insult to injury, on his very first cast he catches a fish - and a big one at that. Don't you feel gutted?

It is all downhill from here as the self proclaimed expert continues to

bag up whilst you catch absolutely Zilch. "Yes another one," he cries after every fish hooked. Then be starts on you; "Not catching much are you mate?" he says sneeringly. Don't you wish he'd just shove the rest of his groundbait in his big mouth and give us all a break?

Never mind, you may even be an expert yourself, one day!

MORE HUMOUR TITLES...

The Ancient Art of Farting by Dr. C.Huff
Ever since time began, man (not woman) has farted. Does this ability lie behind many of the so far unexplained mysteries of history? You Bet - because Dr. C.Huff's research shows conclusively there's something rotten about history taught in schools. If you do most of your reading on the throne, then this book is your ideal companion. Sit back and fart yourself silly as you split your sides laughing! *£3.99*

A Wunch of Bankers
Do you HATE BANKS? Then you need this collection of stories aimed directly at the crotch of your bank manager. A Wunch of Bankers mixes cartoons and jokes about banks with real-life horror stories of the bare-faced money-grabbing tactics of banks. If you think you've been treated badly, read these stories!!!! *£3.99*

The Hangover Handbook & Boozer's Bible
(In the shape of a beercan)
Ever groaned, burped and cursed the morning after, as Vesuvius erupted in your stomach, a bass drummer thumped on your brain and a canary fouled its nest in your throat? Then you need these 100+ hangover remedies. There's an exclusive Hangover Ratings Chart, a Boozer's Calendar, a Hangover Clinic, and you can meet the Great Drunks of History, try the Boozer's Reading Chart, etc., etc. *£3.99*

The Bog Book
(In the shape of a toilet seat)
How much time do you spend in the bog every day? Are you letting valuable time go to waste? Not any longer! Now you can spend every second to your advantage. The Bog Book is packed with enough of the funny, the weird and the wonderful to drive you potty. Fill your brain while you empty your bowels! *£3.99*

MORE GOOD BOOKS...

The National Lottery Book: Winning Strategies

An indispensable guide to the hottest lottery systems in the world. All designed to help you find those lucky lottery numbers that could make you rich.

- Learn how to *Play Like the Pros*... ● Discover ways of *Getting an Edge*...
- Improve your chances with the *'Wheeling Technique'*... ● Find possible ways of *Making it Happen* for you... ● See how understanding betting *Psychology and Equitability* can seriously *Improve Your Winnings*... ● Plus lots more *General Tips* to help you win! £4.99

The Armchair Guide to Football £1.99   **A Load of Bollards** (Cones) £3.99
The Armchair Guide to Golf £1.99   **Down The Pan** (Toilet Humour) £3.99
Rude Cats (Cat Cartoons) £3.99   **The Drinkers IQ Test** £3.99

For a free full colour catalogue of all titles, please send an SAE to the address below.

If you would rather not damage your copy of *The Armchair Guide to Fishing*, please use plain paper and remember to include all the details listed below!

Postage is FREE within the U.K.
Please add £1 per title in other EEC countries and £3 elsewhere.

Please send me a copy of _____

☐ I enclose a cheque/payment made payable to 'Take That Ltd'.
☐ Please debit my Access/Visa card number   Signature:
[ ][ ][ ][ ][ ][ ][ ][ ][ ][ ][ ][ ][ ][ ][ ][ ]   Expiry Date:

Name: _____
Address: _____
_____
_____ Postcode: _____

Please return to: **Take That Books, P.O.Box 200, Harrogate, HG1 4XB**

afish